I0492592

TAKE YOUR BUSINESS ONLINE

THE STEP-BY-STEP GUIDE TO
TAKE YOUR BUSINESS ONLINE
(EVEN IF YOU ARE NOT TECH-SAVVY)

Jahswill StartUP

TAKE YOUR BUSINESS ONLINE

THE STEP-BY-STEP GUIDE TO TAKE YOUR BUSINESS ONLINE (EVEN IF YOU ARE NOT TECH-SAVVY)

Brought to you by StartUP Crest

Copyright 2020 by Eduzobe Jahswill.

All Rights Reserved

No part of this publication may be reproduced, distributed, or transmitted in any forms or by any means, including photocopying, recording, or other electronic or mechanical means without the written express permission of the copyright holder.

This book is part of the business startup guide brought to you by StartUP Crest, a leading business development company with focus on startups and small businesses. You can access more of our resources at startupcrest.com

Contact: info@startupcrest.com +2348033867541

Table of Contents

INTRODUCTION

WHY YOU SHOULD TAKE YOUR BUSINESS ONLINE

So the other day I went to my favorite supermarket to pick up some essentials for the home.

While waiting for the girl at the counter to process my items, I overheard the following conversation:

Man: I honestly don't know how we are going to cope with this lockdown again. My boutique in the market has been locked for weeks now. I missed the Easter sales and my funds are already running out.

Woman: It's terrible for us too oh. I used to sell books and stationeries and back to school packs. As it is now, children may not even be going back to school this year. Where do I start from?

Man: Government has to do something about this lockdown otherwise some of us will die of hunger virus.

Woman: My husband who owns a mechanic workshop is also not allowed to open his shop. They say it's not an essential service. But people still call him to come to their houses to fix minor problems for them. The other day, he was accosted by police and flogged for violating the lockdown. It was by the grace of God that they let him go.

Salesgirl: Aunty, even us oh. See now, it's just the 3 of you that are here now. You know how this place used to be filled in evenings…

The conversations continued with the complaints and lamenting until I left. I kept thinking about what I heard on my way home and was really touched with the way people are suffering in the wake of this pandemic and lockdown.

I kept thinking of how I could have helped those people.

It was right there in my car that it occurred to me that many small business owners don't know how to use the internet to do business.

Many of them don't know that they can take their business online and continue to sell with or without the lockdowns. Imagine if that boutique owner had a website where people can order for clothes, he still would have been selling.

Even that woman's husband who is a car mechanic could still be selling if he tweaked his business model a little bit.

He can record videos on how to fix those minor problems and sell those video recordings to those who call him for the service. His market may even extend to other people.

This thought led me to make a decision:

I am going to help small business owners take their offline businesses online.

Its part of my contribution for the sufferings we are all facing now.

- ✓ You will discover the benefits of taking your business online
- ✓ You will learn if your kind of business can be done online
- ✓ You will learn exactly what and what you need to launch your business online
- ✓ I will also show you the step-by-step process you will take to take your business online.
- ✓ Discover the exact skills you need to run your business online (you probably already have those skills, you just don't know it yet)
- ✓ You will learn the offline business skills that you will bring to your online business
- ✓ You will have the opportunity to ask me any questions at the end of the training.

If you know anyone that may benefit from the training, share it with them.

Invite them to join you on this journey to breaking limits.

This training is to help as many small businesses as possible to take their businesses online.

This is going to be a 5 parts training.

In the first part of the training you will learn how to take an offline business online. I will also cover how to setup a website for free!

In the second part I'll been talking about how to build a website for your business, which you can actually do yourself without spending a dime.

In the third part of the training you will discover how to set up an ecommerce website for business. This will also include how to setup payment gateways so that you can receive payments online.

And in the fourth part you will learn how to manage your online business. The last part of this course will focus on how to grow and scale your online business.

So we're going to begin with part one of this course today, taking a business online. Are you ready?

Earlier, I told you a story of about my encounter at the supermarket.

Do you agree that those people would have benefited from taking their businesses online?

Imagine the supermarket I talked about if they had online display cart. Despite this, pandemic, they probably would have been getting orders online, and will be delivering to their customers, even at home.

They could even store some of the goods in the house since movements are restricted, but non- essential movements are not restricted. Logistic companies who deliver groceries and other things that people need are allowed to move.

So what that means is that if the supermarket had an online presence people could be making orders, anywhere, anytime, and they will just call the logistics company to make the delivery.

So one of the benefits of an online business is the ability to stay active/open and be able to serve your customers 24/7.

Another benefit of an online business is the global reach. People all over the world with internet access can see what you do and patronize you.

In my own business, I've been able to service people from all parts of the world. The first time I had someone from India chat me up to inquire about my services, I couldn't believe it! Only that chat alone gingered my swagger. I was like 'See me oh, all the way from India person they ask for my service'?

In addition to that, setting up an online business is a lot cheaper when it comes to setup cost.

You will not need to rent offices. Pay agency fees, security fees, marching ground, do interior decorations, and so many other things that you would have done with a traditional offline business.

In fact, another way you save costs is having fewer employees. For instance, if you have a traditional offline business, you pay cleaners, security men, and so forth, but for an online business, you don't do all those.

And it also reduces the headache that comes with managing staff; you know that's not easy. Managing staff if you've been in business you know how difficult it is to manage staffs. So having an online business, you reduce that headache for yourself. Abeg, am not saying you should go and fire your staff oh!

One other interesting benefit of an online business is the ability to work from anywhere.

You can work from home.

You can work while traveling. In fact, you can work at your convenience.

As a matter of fact, I am creating this course from my restroom. Yeah, because my little child would not allow me to work in my study.

Being online also affords you the opportunity to compete with the big brands even if you are a small business.

Why?

Because the internet does not know size, so long as you are delivering value no one cares to know if you are working from you room or you have a full estate as your business office.

So, can anyone actually set up an online business? Can any type of business, go online, the answer to both questions is a BIG YES.

Because, online business, it's actually business.

So if the business can be done offline. It can also be done online. I've seen fashion designers online. I've seen artisans, hairstylist big manufacturers, athletes, fitness coaches, professional accountants, lawyers, influencers, Schools, boutiques, restaurant and bars, just name it, any type of business can go online.

CHAPTER ONE

WHAT YOU NEED TO TAKE YOUR BUSINESS ONLINE

So, what do you need to take your Business online?

To help you answer this question, you have to really think of an online business just as an offline business.

To set up an offline business you need a location or street address. You also need an office space.

You want people to see your wares when walking down the street. Maybe a signpost?

So how can you apply this to an online business? Lets try:

Office Space = Website (Note that this can also be a social media page, we will talk more about it)

Address = URL (That is the internet link that people can click to get to your space. For example, one of my addresses is www.bangakitchen.com)

Signpost = Social media accounts (As people are strolling, sorry scrolling on Facebook they will see your space)

P.S

In case you didn't know, when you are scrolling on Facebook or Instagram, you are just like a man walking upandan along the road.

Back to the point…

Bottom-line, you need to have a presence online; somewhere people can come to and always see your business there.

The best presence you can have is a website.

But I know that may sound overwhelming at this time. But not after you see part 2 of this training!

However, if you feel website is too much, you can start with a social media page. Like a Facebook page, Instagram account, LinkedIn account or twitter account.

In fact, you can start with your Whatsapp phone! Yes, you can easily take your business online with your Whatsapp.

Some of you probably heard about this training from my Whatsapp status. Is that correct?

If you first heard about this training from Whatsapp please raise your hand. Yeah.

Again, what we are saying is that you need an online location to take your business online. That location can be a website, social media page/account or even your Whatsapp.

Let me break it down a little by needs:

1. Phone (Smart phone)
2. Internet
3. Social media account/page
4. Domain name
5. Web hosting
6. Free product (Lead magnet)

7. Autoresponder (Or email marketing software)
8. Content
9. Product or service delivery system (Whatsapp, Email account, Private Social media groups, membership website, Google drive, Logistics/courier company)

Let's go to the step by step process of actually taking a business online.

CHAPTER TWO

THE STEP-BY-STEP PROCESS OF TAKING YOUR OFFLINE BUSINESS ONLINE

(WHAT YOU NEED TO TAKE YOUR BUSINESS ONLINE)

STEP 1: PICK A NICHE

So the first thing you want to do is to choose a niche. That is, to select the market that you want to sell to. In doing this, you may want to tweak your existing business.

This step is very crucial because there are so many opportunities online that you can easily get confused. And you want your efforts to be concentrated.

In addition, it's easier to launch when you focus on one small area and grow from there.

That is why you need to drill down to a particular segment of the market which we can call a niche.

For instance, if you sell clothes, it will be best if you first drill down to clothes for dinner outing. Or clothes for beach wears. This way you can stand out in that small niche. The customers will trust you and start raving about your products.

Another reason why it is important to start with a smaller niche is so that you can adapt to what your market needs easily. You can easily satisfy the needs of a small group of people than a larger group.

That way, you can easily communicate with this small group of people who may be able to identify with your business, and you're able to design products and services that this particular niche in this particular market demands, or that they are looking for.

At this point you may also think of tweaking your business offers online.

For example, if you are an Accountant and what you do is small business accounting, you decide that in addition to promoting your services online, you will also teach what you know to small business owners.

In fact, the easiest way to take any offline business online is to teach what you do. If you are a makeup artist, teach how to do makeup, maybe just a face-beat.

If you are a banker, teach people how to save and manage their money. If you are a teacher, teach people how to teach

STEP 2: PICK A PLATFORM

Choose a platform where you will launch – social media or website or messaging app?

If you're doing social media, which of the social media platforms are you going to use. Facebook, Twitter, Instagram, Pinterest, LinkedIn.

To choose a platform you also have to look at your niche. Where is your niche, mostly active? You will not just pick a platform, maybe because you have an account there.

No.

You'll pick a platform where your niche is mostly active.

For instance, many professionals and business to business companies are on LinkedIn.

Thus if you are a professional who is providing professional services maybe like an accountant or a lawyer, LinkedIn will serve you better than if you go to a place like maybe Instagram.

But if you are selling wares, let's say you're selling handmade jewelries you do better on a place like Instagram, because instagramers like pictures. Thus you can take pictures of these and put up.

 If you choose to go the website route, will you do a self-hosted website or use a platform like blogger (not advisable).

You can actually create a website for free, so don't worry about that if money is the problem. I will show you how to do that shortly.

P.S

In the days and weeks ahead, I will organize more free trainings on how you can use each platform to sell more and grow your business as part of this training course.

STEP 3: DEVELOP A STRATEGY

How are you going to reach out to your audience? What are your goals, your objectives? What kind of content do you need to create to attract your desired audience?

So you need to develop a strategy that you will use to be able to send a message that actually resonates with the niche market you have selected. This is very important. And many people tend to neglect it. Taking out time to develop a strategy will really help you to grow your online business.

I will give you a template to help you develop your strategy at the end of the training.

STEP 4: **CREATE SOCIAL MEDIA ACCOUNTS**

Even if you have decided to do the websites route, I will still encourage you to create social media accounts. In fact, if you are taking your business online for the first time, I strongly encourage that you start from social media.

So select the platforms, the platform you selected earlier, create accounts on those platforms. Make sure your accounts and pages are well optimized for business.

Have a good profile picture. A good banner image that tell your audience about what you do. A detailed description of your business, location, opening hours etc...

In a future training, I will teach you how to create an optimized social media page for your business.

STEP 5: **CREATE A LEAD MAGNET**

A lead magnet is something that you can give for free to customers so that they can give you their contacts such as email address or phone number so that you can follow up with them, or for them to like your Facebook page or your Instagram page, or whatever platform you're using but something you can give for free to attract customers.

So your lead magnet could either be an E-book. It could be a course; it could be a checklist, or a quick guide on how to do certain things around your industry. It can also be a free trial of your products/services.

Let me show an example of a lead magnet. Have you noticed that sometimes on the street, people offer you sim cards for free? Why is that so? Anybody knows?

Do you know that there was a time sim cards sold for 50k in this country?!

If you get a free sim card, what will you do with it? Make calls or browse right? Who does that money go to? The network service provider, yes. They gave you a free sim card so that you can become a customer.

Online, this business model is called Freemium. Give something valuable for free, and get paid for a premium advance service or product.

That is what you will need to do too.

A lead magnet also builds trust. Once you use a product and really found it valuable, the next time that person offers you something for sale, you are much more likely to buy than if someone you didn't know before offered that same thing to you.

Why? Because you know that this guy delivers.

So make sure you are giving real valuable lead magnets.

STEP 6: CREATE A LANDING PAGE

A landing page is where people can come to when they want to access your lead magnet. It is sometimes called a squeeze page if used mainly to collect potential customers contact details.

You can use your website to create a landing page. You can also use Facebook in creating a landing page too.

Some email and marketing automation tools (don't worry about the grammar I will explain if you don't know) also give you the means to create landing pages too.

More about all of that later.

Make sure the landing page is created to entice the people that visit it so that they are moved to give you their contact details.

Remember people are weary of giving out their contact details because of security issue; give them something to fear more. Create the fear of missing out (FOMO) on your lead magnet.

STEP 7: START COLLECTING EMAILS

Use your lead magnet on your landing page to collect emails and phone numbers. This will enable you to continuously market your products to these people.

It's important to remember not to bombard your leads with marketing messages. Send them valuable information regularly. Then tactfully promote your offers.

Maybe every 5 free valuable message to one sales offer.

This process of sending such emails can be automatic. Automated to send even while you are doing something else.

The softwares used for doing that are called marketing automation tools.

STEP 8: SETUP YOUR DELIVERY SYSTEM

The means by which you will deliver whatever you are selling to your customers.

If you are selling a physical product, you will need a courier/logistics company to do the delivery for you. There is DHL, Courier plus, NPS Logistics, Wiz Express and so many of them.

Negotiate with them to pick up and deliver to your customers. Even when there is a lockdown they are still allowed to move.

Now you will need to add the delivery cost to your normal sales price.

If you are selling digital products, you can deliver digital products through your website. I don't recommend this though; let your website be for hosting your offers only.

And if you are using only social media, then you can't use this means of course.

What I recommend you use is Google Drive or Dropbox to deliver your digital products.

For instance, my book, **No Bullshit Business Plan,** is hosted on Google Drive. When people pay for the book, they are taken to the link on Google Drive, and they can assess the book from there

You can also use your WhatsApp as a system for delivery.

So let's say you are offering French lessons as a teacher online, you promote them on social media and people pay, you can bring them to a whatsapp group like this one and teach them here.

I have attended trainings on WhatsApp.

Facebook groups, closed groups are another means for delivery trainings and coaching.

Even email accounts too. There is this guy called Emeka Nobis, he is offer trainings where he sends you an email every day for each lesson.

There are a lot of systems; you need to take your time to check them out so that you know what works best for your business.

STEP 9: SETUP PAYMENT GATEWAYS

So people have to pay for them to access a product/service.

You have to set up a system that will allow people to pay you online.

There are lots of payment gateways.

In Africa here the easiest ones to set up are Flutterwave and Paystack. All you need is to create an account, fill your business details and submit your business registration documents and you are set to start receiving payments online.

Even if your business is not yet registered, you can still use the platforms to receive payments online.

To receive International payments with Paystack, you need a Limited Liability Company, RC number. Whereas, this is not required for Flutterwave.

Once they pay, the money will be in your e-wallet and is later transferred to your bank account.

I recorded a video on how to setup Paystack for your business, watch it here.

If you have a registered business name, you can set up a PayPal business account which you can use to receive payments the world over. In another course I'm going to talk about how to set up PayPal to receive payments in Nigeria.

CONCLUSION

QUESTIONS AND ANSWERS

Question 1

So talking about taking offline business online, is it every offline business that can go online? For example I sell sachet water (not bottle that can be supplied to big companies and food outlets like Mr Biggs etc.), and my customers are mainly those that sell sachet water in the streets and along the road, how can I take this online?

Answer

Yes, even if you cannot sell what you are offering online, you can at least connect with your customers online and build greater customer loyalty. Remember, you can also teach what you do online. You can start a social media page that delivers content that your target customers will like.

If your customers are not online, then selling your products online will not be ideal.

Question 2

So I was thinking one of the aims is to get more customers and expand the business, and most of the sachet water sellers don't have android phones.

Answer

How about teaching other potential entrepreneurs how to setup a water factory?

And by the way, I don't agree that your customers are not online.

You will need to be creative and find a way to get your customers social media handles. They are definitely on social media. Once you get a few, you can create buyer personas and run ads that target those buyer personas.

Question 3

Talking about PayPal, do you mean one can receive cash from it even if one did not sell any product online?

Answer

No, you must be selling something or a service.

Question 4

Do I get paid for teaching what I do online?

Answer

Of course! As a laundry person, you can teach people how to press clothes, how to wash colored clothes without fading.

I saw someone looking for this information on Twitter some days ago.

Question 5

So how will one get paid for teaching people how to wash their clothes, or you offer it as a FREEMIUM? How about the fear that if you teach people how to wash colored clothes they won't bring their clothes to you or they will start doing your kind of business?

Answer

There are a lot of ways to do this. Maybe I will do a training on how to get paid teaching people what you know.

Quick one though, package the information in an ebook format like this one and sell it to them.

Question 6

How can school business be done online?

Answer

That is pretty straight forward! Especially in this days of Covid19. You can package lesson plans, scheme of work, assignments etc and deliver all of these over the internet.

We will talk more about this in a later course.

Question 7

Meanwhile, how do i get my business registered in Nigeria? I want to do after d coro era with Jah's help and take my business online immediately

Answer

My wife and business partner is a registered agent with the CAC so she can handle it. You can also do it yourself if you just want to register a business name by visiting this link. Create an account, login and you can do the rest.

However, if you want to register a limited liability company, you cannot do it yourself. That is where my business partner must come in. Contact her here.

Question 8

How do we access more of your free training and videos?

Answer

Visit my websites: www.startupcrest.com and www.bangakitchen.com my social handles are:

YouTube

Facebook

Instagram

Twitter

LinkedIn

Access Part Two Here

Click Me Now!

About the Author

StartUP Jahswill

Entrepreneur | Public Speaker | Business Coach

Eduzobe Jahswill Udogbo (StartUP Jahswill) is a trained Physicist with a passion for building and growing small businesses.

He is the CEO of StartUP Crest, a company he formed to help young people start and grow small businesses.

He is also the CEO of LabHub Medical Laboratories and Diagnostics and the founding Managing Partner/General Manager of Karone Photo World Ltd, both very successful startups.

In 2009 he setup his first registered company, SwiftTech Integrated Solutions Ltd with the aim of providing alternative power supply to residents of the satellite towns around the Nigerian capital territory, Abuja.

Although that venture turned out to be a total failure, Jahswill learned valuable lessons that have helped him to start and grow other businesses with varied degrees of success.

His number one desire is to help as many young people as possible to discover their entrepreneurial skills and use this to start and grow businesses that will provide employment and livelihood.

His mission is simple:

help young people transition from frustrated job seekers and disillusioned startups to successful entrepreneurs.

He promotes financial education that helps young people understand the career options available to them as a means of creating wealth as opposed to the old one-way thinking of "Go to School, get a good job and live comfortably ever after"!

Jahswill appreciates that while university/college education might be a necessity in some chosen careers, it is just one of the options and not the surest path to creating wealth.

That is why he advocates learning business and financial skills that gives the best and surest path to wealth creation.

He spends most of his time developing content for his various educational platforms especially his blog www.startupcrest.com where he provides valuable resources for startups.

He is happily married and blessed with a beautiful daughter.

Books By This Author

Facebook for Business Success: Top Secrets to Help You Run a Successful Business on Facebook

People are buying more products/services online due to the recommendations and promotions they come across on Facebook. A trend that won't die down any time soon.

To market your business successfully on Facebook, you need to understand Facebook's unique opportunities, and how it differs from other media. Just as you wouldn't run a radio jingle on television, you shouldn't market on Facebook the way you'd market in a newspaper or on your website.

This guide will help you do just that!

Social Media Content to Cash: Easily Create Content for Social Media (And Make Money from Your Content)

Over the past 12 years, I have started over 10 businesses with varying degrees of success. I have written several books, one of them is published on Amazon. I have also helped many business owners to start and grow their businesses as part of my consulting business.

In my personal experience as a business person and with many businesses that I have worked with, I have noticed that leveraging the internet is a great way to easily grow your business. However, many business owners don't know how to successfully take a business online.

That is why I created the Facebook group "Take Your Business Online". The goal is to take 1,000 businesses online by end of year 2020. If you are not a member of that group, you should join it. Here is the link to join the "Take Your Busines Online" Facebook group.

From the feedback I have received so far, it has been an amazing success journey. Still, I have also noticed that many who sell online struggle with the number one thing that drives sales and grow your business online - CONTENT!

You see the basic secret to making money whether that is offline or online is to offer value. To solve problems that people have.

People do not buy THINGS; they buy the VALUE (SOLUTION) that the things offer.

You buy a phone, it's because it solves a problem. Maybe it's a communication problem, or the problem of capturing and keeping memories alive. Otherwise, we will still be using a Nokia 3310 today.

People buy clothes not just for covering nakedness, but also for prestige, class, etc.

You must understand this concept if you want to make money.

The thing is if you can offer massive amount of VALUE (SOLUTION) to a huge number of people, you are sure to make it online.

So, whatever you are selling online (products or services) think of it as a VALUE provider, a SOLUTION provider. Knowing this will help you understand the concept of CONTENT 2 CASH.

You will use your CONTENT to provide VALUE and get CASH in return.

People go online for one and one reason alone - CONTENT.

When they open Google, they are searching for content with answers to their questions.

When they open Facebook, they are searching for content about their friends and to express themselves.

When they login to Instagram, they are searching for amazing picture content.

Content drives the internet. The internet was actually created because of content. As a means of organizing content and making it available for anyone, anywhere. That's why content is everything. Some people even say Content is King!

If you have anything to sell online, you must have the ability to create compelling content that pulls in customers and sales. Getting paid for creating quality content should be one of your goals online.

This guide is designed to help you achieve just that: Converting content to cash online.

What You'll Learn

- ✓ Learn how to easily create content posts

- ✓ Discover how to easily come up with content ideas
- ✓ How to legally 'steal' and use other people's content
- ✓ Discover what type of content you should be posting
- ✓ Learn the best time to post so that more people can see your posts (this is GOLD!)
- ✓ Discover the tools that the Pros use to easily create content
- ✓ Discover how to never stress your head again to create content
- ✓ Learn how to create content that sells

Who is This Guide For?

Anyone who has anything to sell online

Social media managers who help other businesses to manage their social media

Business owners who want to take their businesses online

FACEBOOK POSTS ENGAGEMENT SECRETS: 20 Proven Strategies to Get More Likes, Comments and Shares on Your Facebook Posts

It's great that you now have a Facebook business page for your small business (well, if you have not gotten one, this may just be the right time to do so). You may or may not be making sales from Facebook yet. But, you really want to make consistent sales on Facebook.

You have heard about the Facebook algorithm that only posts with high engagement rates tend to do well by reaching more people. Unfortunately, your posts don't get that high engagement. And your sales reflect that.

What do you do?

This guide to the rescue!

FACEBOOK MARKETING MISTAKES: 14 Newbies Mistakes that are Holding Your Business Down

Facebook is one of the highest traffic social media sites in the world. That is, if it is not the highest. It is also the number one social media powerhouse as at the time of producing this guide. With this much clout, is it any wonder that marketers are still clamoring to discover new ways to use this site to generic traffic!

Lots of social media sites continue to pop up every day and gain traction. However, Facebook has continued to dominate the social media market. YouTube, for instance, has grown considerably in recent times. Especially because of the popularity of videos. Facebook remains the number one still.

But marketing on Facebook is not as easy as it seems. To market effectively on Facebook, there are a number of different things you need to be doing. And a lot of people ignore those things or just don't realize how important they are.

The worst still are those who don't know what they shouldn't being doing. They seem to be doing everything right, but fail to see any significant results. The problem?

They are making newbies mistakes that if avoided, can blow their sales through the roof!

In this guide, we are going to learn about some of the biggest mistakes people make when marketing on Facebook. You will discover how to avoid these mistakes and how to turn them around into the most effective marketing campaigns you have ever seen.

NO BULLSHIT BUSINESS PLAN: HOW TO WRITE A BUSINESS PLAN EASILY AND CONVINCINGLY

A simple guide to help you write a great business plan even if you have never done so before.

Used by 100s of people to gain an unfair advantage in positioning their business for success.

Discover why many entrepreneurs are changing the way they look at business planning, and why they are getting the desired results.

IS THIS JUST ANOTHER BUSINESS PLAN WRITING BOOK?

Short answer is NO!

Long Answer: Read on to See How This Book is Different and Will Help You Get Results

Every other business book I have read teaches the old-fashioned business planning way and continues to expand on the idea of the one-page business plan model.

Not this book!

This book introduces you to business planning by first helping you to clarify your purpose of developing a business plan.

You will be introduced to 3 basic rules for writing a successful business plan, break any of these and you may just be wasting your time

Then you will be guided on how to start and complete each section of your business plan.

MORE THAN JUST A BUSINESS PLAN WRITING BOOK

This book takes you above just writing a business plan to learning how to research and validate a business idea.

You will discover how to structure your business and position your offers for success.

In each section, you will see practical examples that explain the point for better understanding.

There are pro tips that your competitors will not be aware us; these can stand your business plan out of the pack.

WHY THIS BOOK WILL BENEFIT YOU

Write a business plan you will be able to implement, not just another document for the drawer.

Complete your business plan in record time.

Avoid 11 of the most common business plan mistakes, make anyone or more of these and your plan may just be trashed!

Write a business plan that bankers and investors will love.

Develop a solid financial business plan with ease and clarity.

NOT JUST ANOTHER AUTHOR

You see, I have written multiple-funded business plans.

Written and pitched business plans that have been selected for grant awards.

Trained other startups and small business owners to apply these strategies with great success.

Started and grown my own businesses, I have always been in the entrepreneurship trenches just like you!.

Written several blog articles on the topic of business planning.

Spoken at seminars and conferences targeted at startups and small business owners.

WHO IS THIS BOOK FOR?

- ✓ Online business owners and startups: Ecommerce store owners, dropshippers, freelancers, affiliates, app developers, website developers, SEOs, etc
- ✓ Traditional business owners and startups: Local businesses such as boutiques, barber shop,

restaurant, farm owners, gym, coffee shop, hair salon, makeup artist, etc
- ✓ Business Managers
- ✓ Aspiring entrepreneurs
- ✓ Entrepreneurship students

WHY YOU SHOULD READ THIS BOOK?

It will make your life a lot easier if you have a business or are planning on starting one.

Even if you think you don't need a business plan now, please read this book. Your views about business planning and business success will change for the better.

Change your business life for the better. Get a copy today!

Make My Day!

Buy a copy of any my books by clicking any of the links below:

Flutterwave (Recommended for Africans)

Amazon (Recommended for Internationals)

www.ingramcontent.com/pod-product-compliance
Lightning Source LLC
Chambersburg PA
CBHW071122220526
45467CB00004B/2018